Over the years my wife and I have used many advent books in anticipation of Christmas. They of course focus on the coming messiah king, but that in turn means they don't focus on the larger picture, the story of God's desire to have a human family and his commitment to that end, and the supernatural conflict in opposition to his plan. *An Advent for the Cosmos* fills that void in a way that's accessible for children and adults. I wish we'd had this years ago.

DR. MICHAEL S. HEISER, Executive Director of the Awakening School of Theology and Ministry, co-host of the Naked Bible Podcast.

An Advent for the Cosmos

Jeffrey Pitts

© 2020 Jeffery Pitts | All rights reserved | Naked Bible Press | ISBN: 978-1-7338497-1-5

Scripture quoted by permission. Quotations designated (NET) are from the NET Bible®
©1996, 2019 by Biblical Studies Press, L.L.C. http://netbible.com All rights reserved

Contents

Introduction

Sometimes things are hidden in plain sight. We may even know they are hidden, but we do not know where to look. That is how I felt in the year of 2018. As my Bible study group was reading through the Bible chronologically, I felt that there were pieces missing from my understanding of topics like idolatry, giants, and the prophetic books.

Ecclesiastes 1:9 states "What exists now is what will be, and what has been done is what will be done; there is nothing truly new on earth.", but yet, I couldn't understand why someone would worship a lifeless token, why I (a Gentile) should care about Israel's rebellion or any number of other passages that I could not explain from my 2000 A.D view of this ancient book.

It was not until my wife, Christi and I took a trip to Africa that I discovered the answer. No, I did not have a revelation, I simply felt more than the culture change when I came back into the U.S. There was a sense of a change that I experienced in spiritual warfare tactics the moment we landed back in the U.S. In Africa, there seemed to be a spirit of fear everywhere, but in the U.S., there seemed to be a spirit of self-pleasure. . Upon mentioning this to my pastor, Douglas A. White, he recommended looking into the work of Dr. Michael Heiser. After watching Dr. Heiser's first two videos on the Naked Bible Podcast 'Start Here' page, I was hooked. The Bible was opened up to me in a totally new way. The overarching story was the same, but I had missed the scope. This was not just about a girl eating a piece of fruit from a tree after being tempted by a snake. Real spiritual warfare had been present from Genesis 3 through Revelation 20. Every biblical author seemed aware of this, but somehow while reading the entire Bible multiple times, I had glossed over these details.

My hope is that this Advent book will expand the scope of your reading of the Bible, show you the extent of rebellion and corruption of God's creation, and convey the need for restoration. It will also trace Jesus' intervention throughout the story and explore the interaction between the visible and invisible worlds.

There are three ways the word "advent" or "coming" applies today: Remembering that Jesus came 2000 years ago to redeem His cosmos, seeing His action through believers every day to demonstrate His kingdom is present now, and knowing that He is coming again as king to complete the restoration of His corrupted creation.

Notes

This book consists of 25 daily Bible studies that are meant to be read starting on December and culminating on December 25th (Christmas). Each day consists of a Bible memory verse, an introduction to the day's topic, a Bible reading, a summary and discussion, questions, a prayer, and a song or songs that correspond with the day's study.

A majority of the advent memory verses will trace the story of faith in Hebrews 11 with other key verses as relevant. A smaller segment of the memory verse has been highlighted for younger children if they cannot memorize the entire verse.

The Bible translation that was chosen for this book is the New English Translation (NET), because of its use of specific English words that facilitate the study.

DAY 1
Creation

Hebrews 11:3, "By faith we understand that the worlds were set in order at God's command, so that **the visible has its origin in the invisible.**"

The visible and invisible worlds are so much bigger than you realize. The main purpose of this advent book is to introduce you to the larger cast of beings in the Bible, to show that Jesus is a major character in the Old Testament, and to trace His story as the Redeemer of the Cosmos (Heaven and Earth). On this first day of advent, we are going to look at several passages from the Bible that do just that, through the story of creation. Pay attention when John calls Jesus the Word.

1

Genesis 1:1: "In the beginning God created the heavens and the earth."

John 1:1–3, 14, "In the beginning was the Word, and the Word was with God, and the Word was fully God. 2 The Word was with God in the beginning. 3 All things were created by him, and apart from him not one thing was created that has been created... 14 And the Word became flesh and dwelt among us, and we beheld His glory, the glory as of the only begotten of the Father, full of grace and truth."

Job 38:4–7, "Where were you when I laid the foundation of the earth? Tell me if you possess understanding! 5 Who set its measurements—if you know—or who stretched a measuring line across it? 6 On what were its bases set, or who laid its cornerstone 7 when the morning stars sang in chorus, and all the sons of God shouted for joy?"

The first verse of the Bible tells us that God created the heavens and the earth. John gives us more details, that the second person of the trinity, Jesus (or the Word), worked with God to create everything! Job then tells us that while God was creating the world through Jesus, "the morning stars" sang together". How can stars sing? They can when "morning stars" is code for angels or spiritual beings! It must have been glorious to hear angels singing together and shouting for joy while Jesus created the heavens and the earth!

Questions

1. Who created the World? God.

2. Who was everything created through? Jesus (The Word).

3. Who sang at creation? "The Morning Stars", another name for spiritual beings or angels.

Prayer

Dear God, you created the world and everything in it, visible and invisible. Help us to sing and shout for joy in your creation today. Amen.

Song

"This Is My Father's World"

DAY 2
Imagers

Hebrews 11:3, "By faith we understand that the worlds were set in order at God's command, so that **the visible has its origin in the invisible.**"

Our memory verse talks about the visible having its origin in the invisible. God, an invisible being, created a visible world, a completely new dimension! After God created the world, He wanted visible stewards to manage it, a second family to image or represent Him physically on Earth. Today, we are going to read about the visible beings Jesus created and commissioned to be His hands and feet in His earthly creation and to expand Eden throughout the Earth.

Genesis 1:1, 26–28, "In the beginning, God created the heavens and the earth." 26 Then God said, "Let us make humankind in our image, after our likeness, so they may rule over the fish of the sea and the birds of the air, over the cattle, and over all the earth, and over all the creatures that move on the earth." 27 God created humankind in his own image, in the image of God he created them, male and female he created them. 28 God blessed them and said to them, "Be fruitful and multiply! Fill the earth and subdue it! Rule over the fish of the sea and the birds of the air and every creature that moves on the ground.""

Genesis 2:8–9a, 15, "The LORD God planted an orchard in the east, in Eden; and there He placed the man he had formed. 9 The LORD God made all kinds of trees grow from the soil, every tree that was pleasing to look at and good for food... 15 The LORD God took the man and placed him in the orchard in Eden to care for it and to maintain it."

Once God created the world, He wanted someone to rule His new creation. Humans were to image God in this new world, being his physical hands and feet, and doing the work He gave them. That work was to "Be fruitful and multiply! Fill the earth and subdue it! Rule over the fish of the sea and the birds of the air and every creature that moves on the ground." God had planted Eden, and humans were commissioned to fill the rest of the earth and make it just like Eden.

Questions

1. What did God create humans as? His imagers, His earthly representatives, His hands and feet.

2. What job or mission did God give His imagers? Be fruitful and multiply. Fill the earth and subdue it (make it like Eden). Rule over the fish, birds, and creatures. (notice that does not include ruling over other humans).

3. How are you imaging God today? How are you His hands and feet? (Help them apply the mission God gave us, e.g. being part of a family, improving the world around them, taking care of nature, pets, animals, working to share with others, etc.).

Prayer

Dear God, you created the world and everything in it. You created us to represent you in the world by taking care of it and Your creatures. Please help us to image you well in this world. Amen.

Song

"This Is My Father's World"

DAY 3
Life in Eden

Hebrews 11:3, "By faith we understand that the worlds were set in order at God's command, so that **the visible has its origin in the invisible.**"

When you think of Eden, what do you imagine? (If you are reading this out loud, have a discussion with everyone about what they think Eden looked like.) Eden was so much more than a grove of trees in which Adam and Eve laid around all day. It was the meeting place of heaven and earth, God's garden. Today, we will learn about what else was in Eden besides trees.

> Genesis 2:8–10, "The Lord God planted an orchard in the east, in Eden; and there he placed the man he had formed. 9 The Lord God made all kinds of trees grow from the soil, every tree that was pleasing to look at and good for food. (Now the tree of life and the tree of the knowledge of good and evil were in the middle of the orchard.) 10 Now a river flows from Eden to water the orchard, and from there it divides into four headstreams."

> Genesis 3:8a, "Then the man and his wife heard the sound of the Lord God moving about in the orchard at the breezy time of the day,"

> Ezekiel 28:13–14, (this is God speaking to a spiritual being) "You were in Eden, the garden of God. Every precious stone was your covering, the ruby, topaz, and emerald, the chrysolite, onyx, and jasper, the sapphire, turquoise, and beryl; your settings and mounts were made of gold. On the day you were created they were prepared. 14 I placed you there with an anointed guardian cherub; you were on the holy mountain of God; you walked about amidst fiery stones."

The pleasant garden of Eden was not just for Adam and Eve. It was "the garden of God". In addition to the orchard described in Genesis, Ezekiel says that it included the holy mountain of God, a place where heaven and earth met. Adam and Eve were also not alone in the garden. Ezekiel says that there were spiritual beings living there: the being addressed in the Ezekiel passage, an anointed guardian cherub, and other spiritual beings referred to as fiery stones. Just like Job referred to spiritual beings as "morning stars", spiritual beings were also commonly referred to as fiery stones. Eden was where God walked and talked with Adam and Eve. That was part of God's plan for His imagers. As we will see in a few days, it did not last, but it must have been wonderful while it did.

Questions

1. Besides a garden, what else was in Eden? The mountain of God.

2. Who else was in Eden besides Adam, Eve, and God? Other spiritual beings (e.g., the one being addressed in the Ezekiel passage, an anointed guardian cherub, and other spiritual beings referred to as fiery stones.)

3. How was life in Eden different from life today? Adam and Eve walked with God, there was no sin, etc.

Prayer

Dear God, it must have been wonderful to live in Your garden. Even though life is not the same today, please help us walk with You by reading Your word and talking to You every day. Amen.

Song

"All Things Bright and Beautiful"

DAY 4
Seeds of Rebellion

Bible Memory

Hebrews 11:6a, "Now without faith it is impossible to please God..."

We have learned that God created the invisible and visible worlds (heaven and earth). These worlds met in Eden at God's holy mountain, surrounded by a beautiful garden. As perfect as it sounds, it did not last. When someone resists authority, it is called "rebellion", and rebellion against God's authority started in the ranks of the spiritual beings in Eden. Remember that spiritual beings are often described as bright or shining. It is also important to know that El is another word for God.

Isaiah 14:12–15,

"Look how you have fallen from the sky, O shining one, son of the dawn!
You have been cut down to the ground, O conqueror of the nations!
13 You said to yourself, "I will climb up to the sky. Above the stars of
El I will set up my throne.
I will rule on the mountain of assembly on the remote slopes of Zaphon.
14 I will climb up to the tops of the clouds;
I will make myself like the Most High!"
15 But you were brought down to Sheol, to the remote slopes of the Pit."

James 4:6b, "God opposes the proud, but he gives grace to the humble."

Isaiah gives us a view into the fall of a spiritual being with a similar description as the spiritual beings referenced in Ezekiel. This spiritual being did not want to be under God's authority. He wanted to rule the Mountain of Assembly in Eden, just like God rules it. But there is only one "Most High" God. This spiritual being's ambition and pride were his downfall. God's word tells us God opposes the proud, and in this passage, He casts down this proud being.

Questions

1. Who rules the mountain of Assembly? God.

2. What is God called in Isaiah 14? (Re-read Isaiah 14:14 if needed) El and The Most High.

3. If God is the Most High, who is He above? Everything, including other spiritual beings.

4. Who does God resist? The proud.

Prayer

Dear God, your word says that you oppose the proud but give grace to the humble. Please help me walk humbly with you. Amen.

Song

"When I Survey the Wondrous Cross" (verse 1)

DAY 5
Human Rebellion
(Forbidden Fruit)

Bible Memory

Hebrews 11:6a, "Now without faith it is impossible to please God..."

When you first learned about Eve talking to the serpent in the garden, you may have had questions like, "Did all animals talk?" or "Why didn't Eve think it was strange to talk to a snake?". Today, we are going to find out why it wasn't weird at all for Eve to be talking to this "serpent", and how it may be related to yesterday's section on the rebellion in Eden.

> Genesis 3:1–7, "Now the serpent was more shrewd than any of the wild animals that the Lord God had made. He said to the woman, "Is it really true that God said, 'You must not eat from any tree of the orchard'?" 2 The woman said to the serpent, "We may eat of the fruit from the trees of the orchard; 3 but concerning the fruit of the tree that is in the middle of the orchard God said, 'You must not eat from it, and you must not touch it, or else you will die.'" 4 The serpent said to the woman, "Surely you will not die, 5 for God knows that when you eat from it your eyes will open and you will be like divine beings who know good and evil." 6 When the woman saw that the tree produced fruit that was good for food, was attractive to the eye, and was desirable for making one wise, she took some of its fruit and ate it. She also gave some of it to her husband who was with her, and he ate it. 7 Then the eyes of both of them opened, and they knew they were naked; so, they sewed fig leaves together and made coverings for themselves."

> Genesis 3: 21–24, "21 The Lord God made garments from skin for Adam and his wife, and clothed them. 22 And the Lord God said, "Now that the man has become like one of us, knowing good and evil, he must not be allowed to stretch out his hand and take also from the tree of life and eat, and live forever." 23 So the Lord God expelled him from the orchard in Eden to cultivate the ground from which he had been taken. 24 When he drove the man out, he placed on the eastern side of the orchard in Eden angelic sentries who used the flame of a whirling sword to guard the way to the tree of life."

In Genesis 3, the Hebrew word translated as serpent, נחש (*nachash*), also has ties with spiritual beings who protect thrones. We have already learned that God's throne was in Eden and there was a cherub guardian there, so it makes sense that it would be normal for Eve to see spiritual beings in Eden. This interaction may have been part of normal life for Adam and Eve. This particular rebellious spiritual being was shrewd though. He did not fight God directly. Instead, he planted doubt in Eve's mind and questioned God's truthfulness. He told her she could be like the spiritual beings she was familiar with in Eden. That may have even been true, but it was not God's plan. He kicked Adam and Eve out of the garden and placed angelic sentries (guards) to guard the way to the tree of life. At this point, God could have killed man, but He did not. Maybe it was even this spiritual being's plan to manipulate God into killing His imagers, but God cannot be manipulated. God chose to provide coverings for Adam and Eve, which required blood to be shed, a foreshadowing of His ultimate plan of redemption.

Questions

1. What kind of being was the Serpent in the Garden of Eden? A spiritual being/ throne guardian.

2. Why was it not weird for Eve to talk with this spiritual being? Spiritual beings lived in Eden. Eve may have talked to them regularly.

3. How did the serpent get Eve to rebel? He questioned God and planted doubt.

4. Once God kicked Adam and Eve out of the garden, how did God keep them out? He placed angelic sentries to guard the way to the tree of life.

Prayer

Dear God, help us to have faith to trust You. We believe that You have given us truth in Your word. Please help us to seek truth in Your word, daily. Amen.

Song

"When I Survey the Wondrous Cross" (verse 4)

DAY 6
Angelic Rebellion
(Mighty Men of Old)

Hebrews 11:6a, "Now without faith it is impossible to please God..."

Have you ever read stories about the Greek gods who met as a council on Mount Olympus? It was from there that the twelve chief gods ruled over the world. What mountain does that remind you of? (The Mountain of Assembly in Eden) There are many myths of how the gods interacted with humans and even had children. Today

14

we will be reading a Bible passage that tells us where those stories of the "mighty heroes of old" came from.

> Genesis 6:1–4, "When humankind began to multiply on the face of the earth, and daughters were born to them, 2 the sons of God saw that the daughters of humankind were beautiful. Thus, they took wives for themselves from any they chose. 3 So the Lord said, "My spirit will not remain in humankind indefinitely since they are mortal. They will remain for 120 more years." 4 The Nephilim were on the earth in those days (and also after this) when the sons of God were having sexual relations with the daughters of humankind, who gave birth to their children. They were the mighty heroes of old, the famous men."

> Jude 6, "You also know that the angels who did not keep within their proper domain but abandoned their own place of residence, he has kept in eternal chains in utter darkness, locked up for the judgment of the great Day."

We (humans) were created as God's earthly imagers, commissioned to fill the earth, and subdue it. Spirit beings were created for the spiritual realm. God was not pleased that the "sons of God" rebelled, leaving the spiritual realm to come to the earthly realm and father their own earthly imagers who were stronger than humans! Their children were called Nephilim or giants, and that is where the myths of mighty heroes of old and famous men came from. If you have ever read the Epic of Gilgamesh, you may have been reading about Nephilim. This epic poem from ancient Mesopotamia is one of the earliest surviving works of literature and describes multiple mighty heroes of old. Not only did humans rebel as we read about yesterday, but even God's angels rebelled against His authority and purpose.

Questions

1. Where were spiritual beings created to live? The spiritual realm.

2. Who was created to image God in the earthly realm? Humans.

3. Where did the mighty men of old come from? Rebellious spiritual beings and their human wives.

4. What did God do with these rebellious angels? He has kept them in eternal chains in utter darkness, locked up for the judgment of the great Day.

Prayer

Dear God, I love You and want to obey You. Please help me obey you. Amen.

Song

"King of Me" (Rend Collective)

DAY 7
Nations' Rebellion
(Tower of Babel)

Hebrews 11:6a, "Now without faith it is impossible to please God..."

Genesis 10 is referred to as the Table of Nations. In it, all the known nations are listed. There were 70 nations, but they all spoke the same language. How is that different from today? (host a discussion on the many languages in the world today and the barriers that causes). As you read the description of the Tower of Babel, think about how it is like the mountain of God in Eden. Then, pay special attention to which family God says are His people.

> Genesis 11:1–8, "The whole earth had a common language and a common vocabulary. 2 When the people moved eastward, they found a plain in Shinar and settled there. 3 Then they said to one another, "Come, let's make bricks and bake them thoroughly." (They had brick instead of stone and tar instead of mortar.) 4 Then they said, "Come, let's build ourselves a city and a tower with its top in the heavens so that we may make a name for ourselves. Otherwise we will be scattered across the face of the entire earth." 5 But the Lord came down to see the city and the tower that the people had started building. 6 And the Lord said, "If as one people all sharing a common language, they have begun to do this, then nothing they plan to do will be beyond them. 7 Come, let's go down and confuse their language so they won't be able to understand each other." 8 So the Lord scattered them from there across the face of the entire earth, and they stopped building the city. 9 That is why its name was called Babel—because there the Lord confused the language of the entire world, and from there the Lord scattered them across the face of the entire earth."

> Deuteronomy 32:7–9, "Remember the ancient days; bear in mind the years of past generations. Ask your father and he will inform you, your elders, and they will tell you. 8 When the Most High gave the nations their inheritance, when he divided up humankind, he set the boundaries of the peoples, according to the number of the heavenly assembly. 9 For the Lord's allotment is his people, Jacob is his special possession."

How was the Tower of Babel like Eden? (Allow some time for answers). Since you know that Eden contained the Mountain of God, where heaven and earth met, it makes sense why the nations of the earth would want to build an artificial mountain, or a tower. It was tall, like the Mountain of God, and its purpose was so they could make a name for themselves, an alternative place to rule from. Genesis tells us that God confused their languages and scattered the nations across the face of the entire earth. Deuteronomy even tells us some more interesting things about this episode. Not only did God divide up humankind, He set their boundaries according to the number of the heavenly assembly. He put spiritual beings in charge of them! Then, He ends Deuteronomy 32:9 by naming his special people, Jacob.

Questions

1. How many nations are in the Table of Nations? 70.

2. How was the Tower of Babel like Eden? It was tall, like the Mountain of God, and its purpose was so they could make a name for themselves, an alternative place to rule from.

3. What did God do to the Nations? Confused their languages and scattered them across the entire earth.

4. Who did God put in charge of the nations? The heavenly assembly (a divine council of spiritual beings).

5. Whom did God choose as his special people? Jacob. We are going to learn more about God's special people tomorrow.

Prayer

Dear God, you alone deserve all of our worship. You alone rule this world. Please help us to follow and worship You instead of ruling our own lives. Amen.

Song

"What A Beautiful Name"

DAY 8
The Call to Abram

Bible Memory

Hebrews 11:8, "**By faith Abraham obeyed when he was called** to go out…without understanding where he was going."

Right after Genesis 11 describes the nations' rebellion against God at the tower of Babel, it introduces us to Terah, Abram's father, Jacob's great-grandfather. As we read yesterday in Deuteronomy 32, the "Lord's allotment is his people, Jacob is his special possession." Of all the people in the world, God chose Abram (later renamed Abraham), the grandfather of Jacob, to be the father of God's select nation,

God's own people. That is what makes the family of Israel different from all the other nations who were assigned members of the Divine Council as their rulers.

Genesis 15:1–6, "After these things the word of the Lord came to Abram in a vision: "Fear not, Abram! I am your shield and the one who will reward you in great abundance." 2 But Abram said, "O sovereign Lord, what will you give me since I continue to be childless, and my heir is Eliezer of Damascus?" 3 Abram added, "Since you have not given me a descendant, then look, one born in my house will be my heir!" 4 But look, the word of the Lord came to him: "This man will not be your heir, but instead a son who comes from your own body will be your heir." 5 The Lord took him outside and said, "Gaze into the sky and count the stars—if you are able to count them!" Then he said to him, "So will your descendants be." 6 Abram believed the Lord, and the Lord considered his response of faith as proof of genuine loyalty."

John 8:56–58, "Your father Abraham was overjoyed to see my day, and he saw it and was glad." 57 Then the Judeans replied, "You are not yet fifty years old! Have you seen Abraham?" 58 Jesus said to them, "I tell you the solemn truth, before Abraham came into existence, I am!"

Hebrews 11:8–16, "By faith Abraham obeyed when he was called to go out to a place he would later receive as an inheritance, and he went out without understanding where he was going. 9 By faith he lived as a foreigner in the promised land as though it were a foreign country, living in tents with Isaac and Jacob, who were fellow heirs of the same promise. 10 For he was looking forward to the city with firm foundations, whose architect and builder is God. 11 By faith, even though Sarah herself was barren and he was too old, he received the ability to procreate, because he regarded the one who had given the promise to be trustworthy. 12 So in fact children were fathered by one man—and this one as good as dead—like the number of stars in the sky and like the innumerable grains of sand on the seashore. 13 These all died in faith without receiving the things promised, but they saw them in the distance and welcomed them and acknowledged that they were strangers and foreigners on the earth. 14 For those who speak in such a way make it clear that they are seeking a homeland. 15 In fact, if they had been thinking of the land that they had left, they would have had opportunity to return. 16 But as it is, they aspire to a better land, that is, a heavenly one. Therefore, God is not ashamed to be called their God, for he has prepared a city for them."

Did you notice Who came to Abraham (= Abram) in Genesis 15:1 ? The Word of the Lord! On day 1, we read who the Word of the Lord was: Jesus! In John 8, Jesus even tells the Judeans about seeing Abraham. The Book of Hebrews tells us that when Abram was called, he had no idea where he was headed, but he trusted and followed God. Also, in Genesis 15, Jesus told Abraham to look at the stars. Then He said to him, "So will your descendants be." Abraham believed Him, and he aspired to a better land, a heavenly one. He looked forward to a restored Eden.

Questions

1. Who came to Abraham? Jesus.
2. What did Jesus tell Abraham his descendants would be like? The stars.
3. How did Abraham show Jesus that he believed? By leaving his home to go to a land he did not know.
4. What was Abraham looking forward to? A heavenly land, a restored Eden.

Prayer

Dear Father, please help me to trust you like Abraham, did. Even though I cannot see heaven today, please help me to trust and follow you. Amen.

Songs

"Father Abraham" and/or "By Faith" (Keith and Kristyn Getty)

DAY 9
Ram in the Bush

Hebrews 11:8, "**By faith Abraham obeyed when he was called** to go out…without understanding where he was going."

After Abraham left his country to follow God, he still did not have a child to fulfill God's promise to make his descendants like the stars. He was becoming old, much older than your grandparents, when God finally provided Abraham's promised son! Abraham was 100 years old! How great this must have been after waiting so long for God to fulfill HIs promise! God always fulfills His promises, although not always by the time we expect. But then, God gave Abraham a test; not like a test you take in school. He tested Abraham by telling him to offer his only son, Isaac, as a burnt offering. Do you think that after waiting 100 years for a child that Abraham would really sacrifice his son? (discuss how difficulty and sad that command would be). Let us find out how Abraham responded in today's lesson.

> Genesis 22:9–14, "9 When they came to the place God had told him about, Abraham built the altar there and arranged the wood on it. Next, he tied up his son Isaac and placed him on the altar on top of the wood. 10 Then Abraham reached out his hand, took the knife, and prepared to slaughter his son. 11 But the Lord's angel called to him from heaven, "Abraham! Abraham!" "Here I am!" he answered. 12 "Do not harm the boy!" the angel said. "Do not do anything to him, for now I know that you fear God because you did not withhold your son, your only son, from me." 13 Abraham looked up and saw behind him a ram caught in the bushes by its horns. So he went over and got the ram and offered it up as a burnt offering instead of his son. 14 And Abraham called the name of that place "The Lord provides." It is said to this day, "In the mountain of the Lord provision will be made."

> Hebrews 11:17–19 "By faith Abraham, when he was tested, offered up Isaac. He had received the promises, yet he was ready to offer up his only son. 18 God had told him, "Through Isaac descendants will carry on your name," 19 and he reasoned that God could even raise him from the dead, and in a sense, he received him back from there."

How much faith would it take to offer up your only son as a burnt offering? Hebrews tells us what Abraham was thinking. He knew that God always keeps his promises, meaning even if God had to raise Isaac from the dead, He would. Even more, pay attention to who called to Abraham. The Angel of the Lord called to Abraham from heaven and referred to Himself as God. We will be learning more about this Angel of God in a couple days.

Questions

1. What did God tell Abraham to do? Sacrifice his son.

2. Why would this have been so difficult for Abraham to do? God had promised Isaac to Abraham, even though he was too old to have children. God also promised that "Through Isaac, descendants will carry on your name."

3. What did Abraham believe that God would do if he had killed Isaac? Raise Isaac from the dead.

Prayer

Dear God, You always keep your promises. Please help me to trust Your word. Amen.

Song

"Standing on the Promises"

DAY 10
Jacob and Bethel

Hebrews 11:8, "**By faith Abraham obeyed when he was called** to go out…without understanding where he was going."

Jacob was Isaac's son, and Abraham's grandson. He did some bad things and was running away from his troubles when he lay down to sleep with a rock for a pillow. While he was sleeping, he had a strange dream. Pay attention to the setting of his dream and see if you recognize anything familiar.

Genesis 28:10–19, "10 Meanwhile Jacob left Beer Sheba and set out for Haran. 11 He reached a certain place where he decided to camp because the sun had gone down. He took one of the stones and placed it near his head. Then he fell asleep in that place 12 and had a dream. He saw a stairway erected on the earth with its top reaching to the heavens. The angels of God were going up and coming down it 13 and the Lord stood at its top. He said, "I am the Lord, the God of your grandfather Abraham and the God of your father Isaac. I will give you and your descendants the ground you are lying on. 14 Your descendants will be like the dust of the earth, and you will spread out to the west, east, north, and south. All the families of the earth will pronounce blessings on one another using your name and that of your descendants. 15 I am with you! I will protect you wherever you go and will bring you back to this land. I will not leave you until I have done what I promised you!" 16 Then Jacob woke up and thought, "Surely the Lord is in this place, but I did not realize it!" 17 He was afraid and said, "What an awesome place this is! This is nothing else than the house of God! This is the gate of heaven!" 18 Early in the morning Jacob took the stone he had placed near his head and set it up as a sacred stone. Then he poured oil on top of it. 19 He called that place Bethel, although the former name of the town was Luz."

Jacob dreamed about a "stairway erected on the earth with its top reaching to the heavens." The last time we saw heaven and earth connected was the mountain of God in the Garden of Eden. The description of the angels walking up and down it and God at the top definitely makes it sound like that is what Jacob was seeing. How fantastic would that be! After Jacob woke up, he named the place Beth-El, "House of El" or "House of God". God promised that someday he would bring Jacob's family back to this land God also reiterated what he had promised to Abraham. He promised that "All the families of the earth will pronounce blessings on one another using your name and that of your descendants." Even as God was selecting an earthly family for Himself, He was revealing how He would use them to reach all the families of the Earth and bless them.

Questions

1. What did Jacob dream about? A stairway from earth to heaven, with angels going up and down it, and God standing at the top.

2. What does this remind you of? The Mountain of God.

3. What did Jacob name the place? Bethel (House of God).

4. Who would eventually live at Bethel? Jacob's descendants.

Prayer

Dear God, thank You for planning how You would bless all the families of the earth through your chosen family of Abraham, Isaac, and Jacob. Please help us to have faith like they did. Amen.

Song

"Forever God is Faithful"

DAY 11
Jacob (Israel)

Hebrews 11:8, "**By faith Abraham obeyed when he was called** to go out…without understanding where he was going."

Eventually, God renamed Jacob to Israel, and his 12 sons became the 12 tribes of Israel. They went through a famine which drove them into Egypt. You can read about that in the story of Joseph (Genesis 37–50).

Today, we are going to read how Jesus shepherded and protected Jacob through all of this. We will read two episodes of Jacob's life where God intervened and Jacob's recognizing Jesus' active role in his life during his blessing of Joseph's sons.

> Genesis 31:10–13, "10 "Once during breeding season I saw in a dream that the male goats mating with the flock were streaked, speckled, and spotted. 11 In the dream the angel of God said to me, 'Jacob!' 'Here I am!' I replied. 12 Then he said, 'Observe that all the male goats mating with the flock are streaked, speckled, or spotted, for I have observed all that Laban has done to you. 13 I am the God of Bethel, where you anointed the sacred stone and made a vow to me. Now leave this land immediately and return to your native land.'"

> Genesis 32:25–30 "Then a man wrestled with him (Jacob) until daybreak. 25 When the man saw that he could not defeat Jacob, he struck the socket of his hip so the socket of Jacob's hip was dislocated while he wrestled with him. 26 Then the man said, "Let me go, for the dawn is breaking." "I will not let you go," Jacob replied, "unless you bless me." 27 The man asked him, "What is your name?" He answered, "Jacob." 28 "No longer will your name be Jacob," the man told him, "but Israel, because you have fought with God and with men and have prevailed." 29 Then Jacob asked, "Please tell me your name." "Why do you ask my name?" the man replied. Then he blessed Jacob there. 30 So Jacob named the place Peniel, explaining, "Certainly I have seen God face to face and have survived."

> Genesis 48:15–16, "Then he (Jacob) blessed Joseph and said, "May the God before whom my fathers

> Abraham and Isaac walked—
> the God who has been my shepherd
> all my life long to this day,
> 16 the **Angel** who has protected me from all harm—
> bless these boys.
> May my name be named in them,
> and the name of my father's Abraham
> and Isaac. May they grow into a multitude on the earth."

As we read in Genesis 31 and 32, God, actively and in person, guided Jacob throughout his life. Then, just before Jacob dies in Egypt, he blesses all his children. While he is blessing Joseph, he makes an incredible statement. "the God who has been my shepherd all my life long to this day, the **Angel** who has protected me from all harm". He refers to the same God of Abraham and Isaac, who shepherded and protected him, as the "Angel who has protected me from all harm"! Here, we see God showing himself bodily to his elect and guiding them according to His plan.

Questions

1. What did the Angel of God tell Jacob in Genesis 31? that He was the God of Bethel and to immediately leave the land he was in and return to his native land.

2. Who did Jacob wrestle within or in Genesis 32? God.

3. What does God change Jacob's name to? Israel.

4. What did Jacob say that God was? His Shepherd and the Angel who protected him.

5. Which person of the Trinity appears in bodily form on earth? Jesus.

Prayer

Jesus, please be near me and guide me like you guided Jacob. Please help me to be faithful to read and obey Your word every day. Amen.

Song

"Jesus is all the World to Me"

DAY 12
Jesus in the Burning Bush

Hebrews 11:27, "**By faith… he persevered** as though he could see the one who is invisible."

After Jacob and his son Joseph died, the Bible tells us that, "Then a new king, who did not know about Joseph, came to power over Egypt." (Exodus 1:8). Egypt enslaved Jacob's family, Israel, for 400 years. The people of Israel cried out to God, and He heard their cry. In today's reading, we learn that God called an Israelite named Moses to lead His people out of slavery. Pay attention to who appeared to Moses in the burning bush in Exodus 3:2.

> Exodus 3:1–5, "Now Moses was shepherding the flock of his father-in-law Jethro, the priest of Midian, and he led the flock to the far side of the desert and came to the mountain of God, to Horeb. 2 The **angel of the Lord** appeared to him in a flame of fire from within a bush. He looked—and the bush was ablaze with fire, but it was not being consumed! 3 So Moses thought, "I will turn aside to see this amazing sight. Why does the bush not burn up?" 4 When the Lord saw that he had turned aside to look, God called to him from within the bush and said, "Moses, Moses!" And Moses said, "Here I am." 5 God said, "Do not approach any closer! Take your sandals off your feet, for the place where you are standing is holy ground."

> Acts 7:30–35, "30 "After forty years had passed, an angel appeared to (Moses) in the desert of Mount Sinai, in the flame of a burning bush. 31 When Moses saw it, he was amazed at the sight, and when he approached to investigate, there came the voice of the Lord, 32 'I am the God of your forefathers, the God of Abraham, Isaac, and Jacob.' Moses began to tremble and did not dare to look more closely. 33 But the Lord said to him, 'Take the sandals off your feet, for the place where you are standing is holy ground. 34 I have certainly seen the suffering of my people who are in Egypt and have heard their groaning, and I have come down to rescue them. Now come, I will send you to Egypt.' 35 This same Moses they had rejected, saying, 'Who made you a ruler and judge?' God sent as both ruler and deliverer through the hand of the angel who appeared to him in the bush."

Did you see what Exodus 3 verse 2 said? The Angel of the Lord appeared to Moses from within the burning bush and then in verse 4, He spoke to Moses. Acts 7 says that "God sent (Moses) as both ruler and deliverer through the hand of the angel who appeared to him in the bush." We will learn more about who this Messenger of the Lord was tomorrow.

Questions

1. The third chapter of Exodus refers to the Mount of God in verse 1. Where else did we see the Mount of God? In Eden.

2. What is special about the Mount of God? That is where heaven and earth meet and God dwells.

3. Who did Moses see in the burning bush? The angel of the Lord.

Prayer

Dear God, thank You for appearing to Moses and delivering Your people. Thank You for saving your people through whom You would send your Son as Savior of all nations. Amen.

Song

"Days of Elijah"

DAY 13

Jesus leads the Israelites to the Promise Land

Bible Memory

Hebrews 11:27, "**By faith... he persevered** as though he could see the One who is invisible."

We do not really think of Jesus as having led the Israelites out of Egypt and into the Promised land, but today, we'll read just a small sample of the passages that tell us He was with His people all along.

Judges 2:1–2, "The Lord's angelic messenger went up from Gilgal to Bokim. He said, "I brought you up from Egypt and led you into the land I had solemnly promised to give to your ancestors. I said, 'I will never break my agreement with you, 2 but you must not make an agreement with the people who live in this land. You should tear down the altars where they worship.' But you have disobeyed me. Why would you do such a thing?"

Joshua 5:13–6:2, "When Joshua was near Jericho, he looked up and saw a man standing in front of him holding a drawn sword. Joshua approached him and asked him, "Are you on our side or allied with our enemies?" 14 He answered, "Truly I am the commander of the Lord's army. Now I have arrived!" Joshua bowed down with his face to the ground and asked, "What does my master want to say to his servant?" 15 The commander of the Lord's army answered Joshua, "Remove your sandals from your feet, because the place where you stand is holy." Joshua did so. 6:1 Now Jericho was shut tightly because of the Israelites. No one was allowed to leave or enter. 2 The Lord told Joshua, "See, I am about to defeat Jericho for you, along with its king and its warriors."

Jude 5, "Now I desire to remind you (even though you have been fully informed of these facts once for all) that Jesus, having saved the people out of the land of Egypt..."

The Lord's angelic messenger leads Israel out of the land of Egypt, and just like at the burning bush, the commander of the Lord's army tells Joshua to remove his sandals, because the place he is standing is holy ground. Then in Jude 5, we find out that this was Jesus, all along, saving His people. Interestingly, Jesus would make this trip again, as a young boy, after His parents fled Bethlehem to escape Herod.

Questions

1. Whom does Judges say lead the Israelites out of Egypt? The Lord's Angelic Messenger.

2. Who defeats Jericho for Israel? The commander of the Lord's army.

3. Whom does Jude say led Israel out of Egypt? Jesus.

Prayer

Jesus, thank you for saving Israel out of Egypt, a trip that you would make again when you came to save us. Amen.

Song

"O Come, O Come, Emmanuel"

DAY 14
Cosmic Geography
(Promised Land/Bethlehem)

Hebrews 11:27, "**By faith… he persevered** as though he could see the One who is invisible."

In 2 Kings 5, there is an interesting story you have probably heard before, about a man from Syria named Naaman. He had leprosy and Elisha told him to wash in the Jordan river seven times. He does not want to wash in the dirty river, but when he finally has faith to obey, God healed him! In today's passage, we are going to focus on something in this passage you've probably missed. Naaman understands who the real God is and has a very strange request of Elisha. We will pick up the story after he is healed.

> 2 Kings 5:15–19, "15 He (Naaman) and his entire entourage returned to the prophet (Elisha). Naaman came and stood before him. He said, "For sure I know that there is no God in all the earth except in Israel! Now, please accept a gift from your servant." 16 But Elisha replied, "As certainly as the Lord lives (whom I serve), I will take nothing from you." Naaman insisted that he take it, but he refused. 17 Naaman said, "If not, then please give your servant a load of dirt, enough for a pair of mules to carry, for your servant will never again offer a burnt offering or sacrifice to a god other than the Lord. 18 May the Lord forgive your servant for this one thing: When my master enters the temple of Rimmon to worship, and he leans on my arm and I bow down in the temple of Rimmon, may the Lord forgive your servant for this." 19 Elisha said to him, "Go in peace."

Remember that in Deuteronomy 32, God not only assigned a divine council member to each nation, but He also set their boundaries. Naaman said that he would worship the Lord alone and no other, but he knew he was returning to enemy territory in Syria. Why did Naaman want enough dirt that it would take two mules to carry? He knew that the God of Israel is the Most High, and he wanted some of His land! Keeping that in mind, we are going to read one more verse about a special place in the promised land.

> Micah 5:2, "But you, O Bethlehem Ephrathah, who are too little to be among the clans of Judah, from you shall come forth for me one who is to be ruler in Israel, whose coming forth is from of old, from ancient days."

Do you remember the lesson about Jacob's dream? Where was he when he dreamt about angels going up and down stairs that reached into heaven? It was Bethel. The area around Bethel is called Bethlehem, and God chose that city to play a special part in receiving His Son.

Questions

1. What was Naaman's strange request? To have a load of dirt to take back to Syria.

2. What was different about the dirt in Israel from the dirt in Syria? It was from God's territory, not from Syria which was ruled by a divine council member.

3. What special event occurred in Bethel that we learned about earlier in this book? Jacob's dream about angels going up and down stairs that reached into heaven with the Lord standing at the top.

4. What is the area around Bethel called? Bethlehem.

5. What special event would happen in Bethlehem? The ruler of Israel whom God would send would be born there.

Prayer

Dear God, the land of Israel is still a special place. Please bless Your land and bless Your people. Please give them peace. Amen.

Song

"Oh Little Town of Bethlehem"

DAY 15
Divine Council Judged

Exodus 20:3, "You shall have no other gods before me."

When God placed the Divine Council in charge of the nations, they were supposed to direct their nation to the true God. They failed miserably, and God judged them in Psalm 82. We have talked about it before, but as a reminder, the name "El" is a Hebrew word for God. You may have heard it used as a name for God, for example, El Shaddai and El Elyon.

Psalm 82, God stands in the assembly of El;

in the midst of the gods he renders judgment.

2 He says, "How long will you make unjust legal decisions

and show favoritism to the wicked? (Selah)

3 Defend the cause of the poor and the fatherless!

Vindicate the oppressed and suffering!

4 Rescue the poor and needy!

Deliver them from the power of the wicked!

5 They neither know nor understand.

They stumble around in the dark,

while all the foundations of the earth crumble.

6 I thought, 'You are gods;

all of you are sons of the Most High.'

7 Yet you will die like mortals;

you will fall like all the other rulers."

8 Rise up, O God, and execute judgment on the earth!

For you own all the nations.

Apparently, the Divine Council was not living up to God's expectation of them, and He chose to judge them. Not only were they making unjust legal decisions: showing favoritism to the wicked, and not defending the poor and fatherless, but they did not teach their nations about the one, true God who owns all the nations. They were "stumble(ing) around in the dark".

Questions

1. What are some of the sins of the Divine Council? Unjust legal decisions, favoritism to the wicked, not defending the poor and fatherless, and not teaching them about the true God.

2. What is their sentence or punishment? They will die like mortals and fall like other rulers.

3. Who owns all the nations? God.

Prayer

Dear God, please help me to make right decisions, show mercy to the poor and fatherless, and to love you and walk with you every day. Please help me to point others to you. Amen.

Song

"Micah 6:8"

DAY 16
Israel's Idolatry

Bible Memory

Exodus 20:3, "You shall have no other gods before me."

After the great faith of Abraham, Isaac, and Jacob you would hope that Israel would stay faithful to the one true God, but it was not meant to be. Idolatry seemed to be Israel's default from the beginning; almost like it was in their nature to abandon God for the spiritual beings that surrounded them. Even as they were being saved from the gods of Egypt, the first generation created a golden calf idol. As you will read today, Israel would continue to abandon God generation after generation.

Exodus 32:1–4, "When the people saw that Moses delayed in coming down from the mountain, they gathered around Aaron and said to him, "Get up, make us gods that will go before us. As for this fellow Moses, the man who brought us up from the land of Egypt, we do not know what has become of him!" So, Aaron said to them, "Break off the gold earrings that are on the ears of your wives, your sons, and your daughters, and bring them to me." So all the people broke off the gold earrings that were on their ears and brought them to Aaron. He accepted the gold from them, fashioned it with an engraving tool, and made a molten calf. Then they said, "These are your gods, O Israel, who brought you up out of Egypt.""

Deuteronomy 32:17, "They sacrificed to demons, not God, to gods they had not known; to new gods who had recently come along, gods your ancestors had not known about."

Judges 2:10–15, "That entire generation passed away; a new generation grew up that had not personally experienced the Lord's presence or seen what he had done for Israel. 11 The Israelites did evil before the Lord by worshiping the Baals. 12 They abandoned the Lord God of their ancestors who brought them out of the land of Egypt. They followed other gods—the gods of the nations who lived around them. They worshiped them and made the Lord angry. 13 They abandoned the Lord and worshiped Baal and the Ashtoreths. 14 The Lord was furious with Israel and handed them over to robbers who plundered them. He turned them over to their enemies who lived around them. They could not withstand their enemies' attacks. 15 Whenever they went out to fight, the Lord did them harm, just as he had warned and solemnly vowed, he would do. They suffered greatly."

Just like God created humans to image Him on earth, people made things called idols to image the divine beings they wanted to worship. They even had ceremonies that invited the spiritual being to inhabit the idol or image. You will ind that there are many things in the world that are poor, twisted copies of the wonderful things that God created in the beginning. That is why God's second commandment was, "You shall not make for yourself a carved image or any likeness of anything that is in heaven above or that is on the earth beneath or that is in the water below. You shall not bow down to them or serve them, for I, the Lord, your God, am a jealous God, responding to the transgression of fathers by dealing with children to the third and fourth generations of those who reject me, and showing covenant faithfulness to a thousand generations of those who love me and keep my commandments." (Exodus 20:4–6)

Questions

1. What did God create as His imagers? Humans.

2. What did Israel make to be the image of spiritual beings? Idols

3. Which commandment forbids humans from creating and worshiping images? The second (Exodus 20:4–6).

4. What things can distract us from serving God now? Entertainment, video games, popularity, possessions, etc.

Prayer

Dear God, thank you for creating us as your imagers on earth. Please make us more and more like Jesus, so that we can image You well. Help us to not be distracted from serving You alone. Amen.

Song

"Give us Clean Hands"

DAY 17
Ruth the Moabite

Bible Memory

Hebrews 11:33, "**Through faith they** conquered kingdoms, administered justice, **gained what was promised**, shut the mouths of lions,"

E ven though Israel was God's chosen people, He still included people from other nations in His plan to send His Son to earth. In today's passage from the Bible, we will learn about one of those Gentiles that God brought to faith and used in His plan. While you are reading, remember what we learned about cosmic geography. By leaving Judah to move to Moab, Elimelech and Naomi were leaving God's territory.

Also, pay attention to Naomi's reference to the god in Moab vs. Ruth's reference to the true God.

> Ruth 1:1–19, "During the time of the judges there was a famine in the land of Judah. So, a man from Bethlehem in Judah went to live as a resident foreigner in the region of Moab, along with his wife and two sons. 2 (Now the man's name was Elimelech, his wife was Naomi, and his two sons were Mahlon and Kilion. They were of the clan of Ephrath from Bethlehem in Judah.) They entered the region of Moab and settled there. 3 Sometime later Naomi's husband Elimelech died, so she and her two sons were left alone. 4 So her sons married Moabite women. (One was named Orpah and the other Ruth.) And they continued to live there about ten years. 5 Then Naomi's two sons, Mahlon and Kilion, also died. So, the woman was left all alone—bereaved of her two children as well as her husband! 6 So she decided to return home from the region of Moab, accompanied by her daughters-in-law, because while she was living in Moab she had heard that the Lord had shown concern for his people, reversing the famine by providing abundant crops. 7 Now as she and her two daughters-in-law began to leave the place where she had been living to return to the land of Judah, 8 Naomi said to her two daughters-in-law, "Listen to me! Each of you should return to your mother's home! May the Lord show you the same kind of devotion that you have shown to your deceased husbands and to me! 9 May the Lord enable each of you to find security in the home of a new husband!" Then she kissed them goodbye and they wept loudly. 10 But they said to her, "No! We will return with you to your people." 11 But Naomi replied, "Go back home, my daughters! There is no reason for you to return to Judah with me! I am no longer capable of giving birth to sons who might become your husbands! 12 Go back home, my daughters! For I am too old to get married again. Even if I thought that there was hope that I could get married tonight and conceive sons, 13 surely you would not want to wait until they were old enough to marry! Surely you would not remain unmarried all that time! No, my daughters, you must not return with me. For my intense suffering is too much for you to bear. For the Lord is afflicting me!" 14 Again they wept loudly.

Then Orpah kissed her mother-in-law goodbye, but Ruth clung tightly to her. 15 So Naomi said, "Look, your sister-in-law is returning to her people and to her god. Follow your sister-in-law back home!" 16 But Ruth replied, "Stop urging me to abandon you! For wherever you go, I will go. Wherever you live, I will live. Your people will become my people, and your God will become my God. 17 Wherever you die, I will die—and there I will be buried. May the Lord punish me severely if I do not keep my promise! Only death will be able to separate me from you!" 18 When Naomi realized that Ruth was determined to go with her, she stopped trying to dissuade her. 19 So the two of them journeyed together until they arrived in Bethlehem.

In verse 16, Ruth shows the faith she has in God by saying that Naomi's God will be her God. Later in the book of Ruth, we learn that she was married into the nation of Israel through Boaz, her kinsman redeemer. He is a shadow of Jesus later redeeming us and making us part of His family. Later on, in Matthew 1:5–6, we learn that they had a son named Obed who became the grandfather of King David! The genealogical list in Matthew is important, because it is a record of the family of Jesus!

Questions

1. Was Ruth born into Israel or another nation? Another nation.

2. What changed for Ruth when she stayed with Naomi? She traded her gods for the true God and moved from their territory to His.

3. How did God use her in His Son's earthly family? She was the great grandmother of King David.

Prayer

Dear God, thank you for being our God and bringing us into your family. Help us to tell others about You as our Redeemer and to welcome them into your family. Amen.

Song

"I Will Follow" (Chris Tomlin)

DAY 18
King David's Throne

Hebrews 11:33, "**Through faith they** conquered kingdoms, administered justice, **gained what was promised**, shut the mouths of lions,"

In today's lesson, God promises King David an amazing thing, an eternal dynasty, a throne forever. But how could a king who would die reign forever? Let us find out.

Psalm 89:1–27, "I will sing continually about the Lord's faithful deeds; to future generations I will proclaim your faithfulness. 2 For I say, "Loyal love is permanently established; in the skies you set up your faithfulness." 3 The Lord said, "I have made a covenant with my chosen one; I have made a promise on oath to David, my servant: 4 'I will give you an eternal dynasty and establish your throne throughout future generations.'" (Selah) 5 O Lord, the heavens praise your amazing deeds, as well as your faithfulness in the angelic assembly. 6 For who in the skies can compare to the Lord? Who is like the Lord among the heavenly beings, 7 a God who is honored in the great angelic assembly, and more awesome than all who surround him? 8 O Lord, sovereign God! Who is strong like you, O Lord? Your faithfulness surrounds you. 9 You rule over the proud sea. When its waves surge, you calm them. 10 You crushed the Proud One and killed it; with your strong arm you scattered your enemies. 11 The heavens belong to you, as does the earth. You made the world and all it contains. 12 You created the north and the south. Tabor and Hermon rejoice in your name. 13 Your arm is powerful, your hand strong, your right hand victorious. 14 Equity and justice are the foundation of your throne. Loyal love and faithfulness characterize your rule. 15 How blessed are the people who worship you! O Lord, they experience your favor. 16 They rejoice in your name all day long, and are vindicated by your justice. 17 For you give them splendor and strength. By your favor we are victorious. 18 For our shield belongs to the Lord, our king to the Holy One of Israel. 19 Then you spoke through a vision to your faithful followers and said: "I have energized a warrior; I have raised up a young man from the people. 20 I have discovered David, my servant. With my holy oil I have anointed him as king. 21 My hand will support him, and my arm will strengthen him. 22 No enemy will be able to exact tribute from him; a violent oppressor will not be able to humiliate him. 23 I will crush his enemies before him; I will strike down those who hate him. 24 He will experience my faithfulness and loyal love, and by my name he will win victories. 25 I will place his hand over the sea, his right hand over the rivers. 26 He will call out to me, 'You are my father, my God, and the protector who delivers me.' 27 I will appoint him to be my firstborn son, the most exalted of the earth's kings. 28 I will always extend my loyal love to him, and my covenant with him is secure. 29 I will give him an eternal dynasty, and make his throne as enduring as the skies above. 30 If his sons reject my law and disobey my regulations, 31 if they break my rules and do not keep my commandments, 32 I will punish their rebellion by beating them with a club, their sin by inflicting them with bruises. 33 But I will not remove my loyal love from him, nor be unfaithful to my promise. 34 I will not break my covenant or go back on what I promised. 35 Once and for all I have vowed by my own holiness, I will never deceive David. 36 His dynasty will last forever. His throne will endure before me, like the sun, 37 it will remain stable, like the moon, his throne will endure like the skies." (Selah)

Acts 2:34–36, "For David did not ascend into heaven, but he himself says, 'The Lord said to my lord, " Sit at my right hand until I make your enemies a footstool for your feet."' Therefore, let all the house of Israel know beyond a doubt that God has made this Jesus whom you crucified both Lord and Christ."

God gave King David an eternal dynasty, which means that his sons and their sons would always reign on the throne. Then in verses 8–18, David describes what the rule of the Lord is like, using phrases like, "Equity and justice are the foundation of your throne." and "Loyal love and faithfulness characterize your rule." One of King David's descendants would be Jesus, that is how his dynasty would last forever. In Acts, Peter declared that Jesus was on the Throne! And His reign would be the opposite of how the fallen Divine Council reigned. God would put the world back into order.

Questions

1. What is a dynasty? A king's family who reigns one after another.

2. How long did God promise that David's dynasty would last? Forever

3. Who would be the final King forever? Jesus.

4. What are some things that His kingdom would have? Equity, justice, love, and faithfulness.

Prayer

Dear God, we look forward to living in Your Kingdom, when Your Son, King David's heir, rules with equity and justice, love, and faithfulness. What a blessed kingdom that will be! Amen.

Song

"Before the Throne of God Above"

DAY 19
Daniel, Leader of Wise Men

Bible Memory

Hebrews 11:33, "**Through faith they** conquered kingdoms, administered justice, **gained what was promised**, shut the mouths of lions,"

The book of Daniel starts with a young boy from Judah who was captured and taken to Babylon during God's punishment of Israel for not obeying His laws.

They trained him and his friends in the mystic ways of Babylon, but he stayed faithful to God, and God used him in mighty ways.

Daniel 2:1–13, "In the second year of his reign Nebuchadnezzar had many dreams. His mind was disturbed, and he suffered from insomnia. 2 The king issued an order to summon the magicians, astrologers, sorcerers, and wise men in order to explain his dreams to him. So they came and awaited the king's instructions. 3 The king told them, "I have had a dream, and I am anxious to understand the dream." 4 The wise men replied to the king: [What follows is in Aramaic] "O king, live forever! Tell your servants the dream, and we will disclose its interpretation." 5 The king replied to the wise men, "My decision is firm. If you do not inform me of both the dream and its interpretation, you will be dismembered, and your homes reduced to rubble! 6 But if you can disclose the dream and its interpretation, you will receive from me gifts, a reward, and considerable honor. So disclose to me the dream and its interpretation!" 7 They again replied, "Let the king inform us of the dream; then we will disclose its interpretation." 8 The king replied, "I know for sure that you are attempting to gain time, because you see that my decision is firm. 9 If you don't inform me of the dream, there is only one thing that is going to happen to you. For you have agreed among yourselves to report to me something false and deceitful until such time as things might change. So tell me the dream, and I will have confidence that you can disclose its interpretation." 10 The wise men replied to the king, "There is no man on earth who is able to disclose the king's secret, for no king, regardless of his position and power, has ever requested such a thing from any magician, astrologer, or wise man. 11 What the king is asking is too difficult, and no one exists who can disclose it to the king, except for the gods—but they don't live among mortals!" 12 Because of this the king got furiously angry and gave orders to destroy all the wise men of Babylon. 13 So a decree went out, and the wise men were about to be executed. They also sought Daniel and his friends so that they could be executed."

Daniel 2:24, "Then Daniel went in to see Arioch (whom the king had appointed to destroy the wise men of Babylon). He came and said to him, "Don't destroy the wise men of Babylon! Escort me to the king, and I will disclose the interpretation to him!'"

Daniel 2:44–49, "In the days of those kings the God of heaven will raise up an everlasting kingdom that will not be destroyed and a kingdom that will not be left to another people. It will break in pieces and bring about the demise of all these kingdoms. But it will stand forever. 45 You saw that a stone was cut from a mountain, but not by human hands; it smashed the iron, bronze, clay, silver, and gold into pieces. The great God has made known to the king what will occur in the future. The dream is certain, and its interpretation is reliable." 46 Then King Nebuchadnezzar bowed down with his face to the ground and paid homage to Daniel. He gave orders to offer sacrifice and incense to him. 47 The king replied to Daniel, "Certainly your God is a God of gods and Lord of kings and revealer of mysteries, for you were able to reveal this mystery!" 48 Then the king elevated Daniel to high position and bestowed on him many marvelous gifts. He granted him authority over the entire province of Babylon and made him the main prefect over all the wise men of Babylon. 49 And at Daniel's request, the king appointed Shadrach, Meshach, and Abednego over the administration of the province of Babylon. Daniel himself served in the king's court."

When the king wanted to test his wise men, the stakes were high. The king wanted them to tell him his dream and the meaning. The king gave orders to kill the wise men, because they could not tell him his dream. Their excuse was, "Only the gods (spiritual beings) know that!" Since Daniel trusted the one true God, he was able to tell the king his dream and its interpretation. In the dream, a large stone that represents the Kingdom of God crushes the kingdoms of the earth. As a reward for telling the dream and its interpretation, King Nebuchadnezzar made Daniel the ruler over his wise men. Remember the wise men because they show up later in this grand story.

Questions

1. What did King Nebuchadnezzar want his wise men to do? Tell him his dream and what it meant.

2. Who did his wise men tell him were the only ones who could tell him his dream? The gods (spiritual beings).

3. Who was able to tell the king his dream and its interpretation? Daniel

4. What does the stone in the dream represent? God's everlasting kingdom that will bring down all other kingdoms.

5. To which position does King Nebuchadnezzar appoint Daniel? Ruler over the wise men.

Prayer

Dear God, thank you for using bad situations for good, like Israel's exile to Babylon. Please help me to trust you like Daniel and to speak the truth. Amen.

Songs

"King of Me" (Rend Collective), "By Faith" (Gettys)

DAY 20
God's Grace of a Remnant

Bible Memory

Romans 11:5, "So in the same way at the present time **there is a remnant chosen by grace.**"

With so many rebellions against God: spiritual beings, humans, and the nations, how could God possibly save His cosmos without destroying it and starting over? The answer is that He chose remnants to implement His plan of saving the Cosmos. A remnant is "a small remaining quantity of something", and as our Bible memory verse states, "there is a remnant, chosen by grace." Today, we will be looking at an example of God saving a remnant for His own purpose.

Romans 11:1–6, "So I ask, God has not rejected his people, has he? Absolutely not! For I too am an Israelite, a descendant of Abraham, from the tribe of Benjamin. 2 God has not rejected his people whom he foreknew! Do you not know what the scripture says about Elijah, how he pleads with God against Israel? 3 "Lord, they have killed your prophets, they have demolished your altars; I alone am left and they are seeking my life!" 4 But what was the divine response to him? "I have kept for myself seven thousand people who have not bent the knee to Baal." 5 So in the same way at the present time there is a remnant chosen by grace. 6 And if it is by grace, it is no longer by works, otherwise grace would no longer be grace."

In Romans, Paul gives us an example from the Old Testament when even God's chosen prophet, Elijah, despaired at the condition of Israel, God's chosen people. Elijah thought he was alone in Israel as the only person serving God. What he did not know is that God had done a miraculous thing and saved seven thousand people that still served the one true God. I am sure that those were encouraging words indeed. Over the next three days, we are going to look at God's remnants throughout the cosmos which God used to bring salvation to the world.

Questions

1. Which prophet was discouraged and thought he was the only one left in Israel to serve God? Elijah.

2. How many Israelites still served God alone that God had protected? 7,000.

3. Why and how does God choose to save people, even though they don't deserve it? He has grace.

4. Does God still have a remnant today? Yes.

Prayer

Dear God, thank you for choosing a remnant by grace. It is your grace that has made salvation possible. Amen.

Song

"The Holy Remnant" (https://hymnary.org/text/are_you_of_the_holy_remnant)

DAY 21
Human Remnant
(Mary's Obedience)

Romans 11:5, "So in the same way at the present time **there is a remnant chosen by grace.**"

When Adam and Eve chose to rebel against God by not trusting His word and eating the forbidden fruit, He could have abandoned them and their ancestors to their fate. Instead, He chose to maintain a remnant. In Genesis 3, He even promised to send someone through the offspring of Eve that would crush the head of the enemy. God had grace on humans by maintaining a remnant. Today's reading is about the human remnant, a young girl from Nazareth, whom God used to fulfill His promise to Eve.

> Luke 1:26–38, "26 In the sixth month of Elizabeth's pregnancy, the angel Gabriel was sent by God to a town of Galilee called Nazareth, 27 to a virgin engaged to a man whose name was Joseph, a descendant of David, and the virgin's name was Mary. 28 The angel came to her and said, "Greetings, favored one, the Lord is with you!" 29 But she was greatly troubled by his words and began to wonder about the meaning of this greeting. 30 So the angel said to her, "Do not be afraid, Mary, for you have found favor with God! 31 Listen: You will become pregnant and give birth to a son, and you will name him Jesus. 32 He will be great and will be called the Son of the Most High, and the Lord God will give him the throne of his father David. 33 He will reign over the house of Jacob forever, and his kingdom will never end." 34 Mary said to the angel, "How will this be, since I have not had sexual relations with a man?" 35 The angel replied, "The Holy Spirit will come upon you, and the power of the Most High will overshadow you. Therefore, the child to be born will be holy; he will be called the Son of God. 36 "And look, your relative Elizabeth has also become pregnant with a son in her old age—although she was called barren, she is now in her sixth month! 37 For nothing will be impossible with God." 38 So Mary said, "Yes, I am a servant of the Lord; let this happen to me according to your word." Then the angel departed from her."

Did you notice who verse 27 said Mary was a descendant of? King David! God maintained a human remnant from Eve to Abraham to King David to Mary. Much of the story of the Old Testament traces God's intervention to maintain a human remnant that He would eventually use to send His Son to earth.

Remember that God had promised King David an "eternal dynasty". Mary was told that she would have a son, and that He would be great, and called the Son of the Most High, and the Lord God would give him the throne of his father David. Can you imagine how overwhelming that would be? But Mary reacted differently than Eve. Mary had faith and responded in obedience.

Questions

1. Who did God send to tell Mary that she would have a son? An angel named Gabriel.

2. What would her son be called? Son of the Most High.

3. What would God give Him? The throne of his father, David.

4. How was Mary's response different from Eve's response? Mary believed God, had faith, and responded in obedience.

Prayer

Dear God, thank you for choosing to send your Son as a baby who would one day be King and save us as His Remnant. Thank you for the faith and obedience that you gave Mary. Please help us to respond to you in faith and obedience. Amen.

Song

"The Holy Remnant"

DAY 22
Angelic Remnant
(Angels' Announcement)

Romans 11:5, "So in the same way at the present time **there is a remnant chosen by grace.**"

C an you remember the three days in which we learned about spiritual beings rebelling? (Give some time for guesses) The first was a throne guardian that rebelled in the garden and deceived Adam and Eve into eating the forbidden fruit.

The second was when the sons of God rebelled by leaving their realm, taking human wives, and producing giants. The third was when some members of the Divine Council rebelled against their purpose of leading their nations to God, and they replaced Him with idols to themselves. Today, we will see that God kept a remnant in the spiritual realm, and a whole host of spiritual beings sang at the coming of the Redeemer.

> Luke 2:8–15, "8 Now there were shepherds nearby living out in the field, keeping guard over their flock at night. 9 An angel of the Lord appeared to them, and the glory of the Lord shone around them, and they were absolutely terrified. 10 But the angel said to them, "Do not be afraid! Listen carefully, for I proclaim to you good news that brings great joy to all the people: 11 Today your Savior is born in the city of David. He is Christ the Lord. 12 This will be a sign for you: You will find a baby wrapped in strips of cloth and lying in a manger." 13 Suddenly a vast, heavenly army appeared with the angel, praising God and saying, 14 "Glory to God in the highest, and on earth peace among people with whom he is pleased!" 15 When the angels left them and went back to heaven, the shepherds said to one another, "Let us go over to Bethlehem and see this thing that has taken place, that the Lord has made known to us."

It would be easy to think that all spiritual beings had rebelled, but just like God kept a human remnant, He also kept a spirit remnant as well! The word 'angel' literally means 'messenger'. What a privilege it was for these spiritual beings to be God's messengers to the shepherds and tell them about the Savior being born on Earth. I wonder if this chorus of Angels who sang at Jesus' birth was the same group that we read about on Day 1, who sang at creation? This time, there were humans listening, and they believed! The Shepherds were excited to see their Savior, born on earth!

Questions

1. What does the word 'Angel' mean? Messenger.

2. What two events in the Bible have we read that describe spiritual beings singing? At creation and when announcing the birth of Jesus.

3. How did the Shepherds respond to the message by faith? They believed God's messengers and went to Bethlehem to see the new baby.

Prayer

Dear God, thank you for choosing to send your Son as a baby, who would one day be King and save us as His remnant. Thank you for sending your messengers to the shepherds and giving them faith to believe. Please help us to respond to you in faith. Amen.

Songs

"Hark the Herald Angels Sing", "Angels We have Heard on High"

DAY 23
Nations' Remnant
(Daniel's Legacy, The Wise Men)

Romans 11:5, "So in the same way at the present time **there is a remnant chosen by grace.**"

Even though the nations rebelled against God at the tower of Babel, and He turned them over to be ruled by the Divine Council, God did not abandon the Gentiles (people who are not part of Israel). He had a plan for including them in the celebration of His Son's birth.

> Daniel 2:47–48, "The king replied to Daniel, "Certainly your God is a God of gods and Lord of kings and revealer of mysteries, for you were able to reveal this mystery!" 48 Then the king elevated Daniel to high position and bestowed on him many marvelous gifts. He granted him authority over the entire province of Babylon and made him the main prefect over all the wise men of Babylon."

> Matthew 2:1–12, "Now after Jesus was born in Bethlehem of Judea in the days of Herod the king, behold, wise men from the East came to Jerusalem, 2 saying, "Where is He who has been born King of the Jews? For we have seen His star in the East and have come to worship Him." 3 When Herod the king heard this, he was troubled, and all Jerusalem with him. 4 And when he had gathered all the chief priests and scribes of the people together, he inquired of them where the Christ was to be born. 5 So they said to him, "In Bethlehem of Judea, for thus it is written by the prophet: 6 'But you, Bethlehem, in the land of Judah, Are not the least among the rulers of Judah; For out of you shall come a Ruler Who will shepherd My people Israel.' " 7 Then Herod, when he had secretly called the wise men, determined from them what time the star appeared. 8 And he sent them to Bethlehem and said, "Go and search carefully for the young Child, and when you have found Him, bring back word to me, that I may come and worship Him also." 9 When they heard the king, they departed; and behold, the star which they had seen in the East went before them, till it came and stood over where the young Child was. 10 When they saw the star, they rejoiced with exceedingly great joy. 11 And when they had come into the house, they saw the young Child with Mary His mother, and fell down and worshiped Him. And when they had opened their treasures, they presented gifts to Him: gold, frankincense, and myrrh. 12 Then, being divinely warned in a dream that they should not return to Herod, they departed for their own country another way."

Where do you suppose the Wise Men learned about the coming Messiah, King of the Jews? (Give some time for answers) Daniel, whom King Nebuchadnezzar appointed as the leader of the wise men of Babylon is a big possibility. Do you suppose that these wise men, who traveled to see the new King of the Jews, grew up reading Daniel or Ezekiel, who both lived and wrote in Babylon during Israel's exile there? Later, Paul the Apostle, would write in Ephesians 3:6 that "through the gospel, the Gentiles are fellow heirs, fellow members of the body, and fellow partakers of the promise in Christ Jesus." What wonderful news it is that God has included Gentiles in the promise of Christ Jesus!

Questions

1. What prophet was placed in charge of the wise men of Babylon? Daniel.

2. Does the Bible tell us how many wise men visited Jesus? No. But it does tell us that they brought three gifts (Gold, Frankincense, and Myrrh).

3. How are Gentiles (people who are not part of Israel) part of the body of Christ? Through the gospel.

Prayer

Thank you God for including Gentiles in Your plan for celebrating the birth of your son and thank you that You have promised that all nations will stand before Your throne and praise You. Amen.

Songs

"We Three Kings", "All Hail the Power of Jesus' Name"

DAY 24

For God so Loved the Cosmos

John 3:16: "For **this is the way God loved the [Cosmos]**: He gave his one and only Son, so that everyone who believes in him will not perish but have eternal life."

A s we have seen throughout this Advent study, humans were not the only thing that needed redemption. Everything had been corrupted: throne guardians, humans, plants, animals, nations, and the Divine Council. Today, we will see how

God described His creation as groaning, waiting to be redeemed and His plan to redeem it all.

> Romans 8:19–22 "For the creation eagerly waits for the revelation of the sons of God. 20 For the creation was subjected to futility—not willingly but because of God who subjected it—in hope 21 that the creation itself will also be set free from the bondage of decay into the glorious freedom of God's children. 22 For we know that the whole creation groans and suffers together until now."

> John 3:16: "For this is the way God loved the [cosmos]: He gave his one and only Son, so that everyone who believes in him will not perish but have eternal life."

As Romans tells us, all of creation groans and suffers. All the violence in creation (humans, animals, and spiritual beings) is evidence that things are not right. But one day, God will set creation free from that bondage. Even one of the most well-known verses, John 3:16, says that because God loved the cosmos (which includes humans), He sent His one and only Son. He is the one for which the cosmos has been waiting.

Questions

1. List some things that we have learned were corrupted. Throne guardians, humans, plants, animals, nations, and the Divine Council.
2. What does Romans say groans, waiting to be set free? All of creation.
3. In John 3:16, what does God love? The Cosmos.
4. Does that include us (humans)? Yes!

Prayer

Dear God, thank you for not abandoning Your creation. You had a plan all along that no one could stop, and eventually, we will see everything redeemed in Your new Kingdom. Amen.

Song

"Joy to the World"

DAY 25
The Birth of The Savior

John 3:16: "For **this is the way God loved the [Cosmos]**: He gave his one and only Son, so that everyone who believes in him will not perish but have eternal life."

All of history had been leading up to and waiting for the Messiah to come to earth. Everything was ready in God's plan to redeem the cosmos. His remnant family was traveling to the prophesied birth city, the star announcing His birth was informing a remnant of Gentiles of his coming, and a remnant of spiritual beings were ready to sing of the birth. Today, we will read about His birth.

Luke 2:1–7, "Now in those days a decree went out from Caesar Augustus to register all the empire for taxes. 2 This was the first registration, taken when Quirinius was governor of Syria. 3 Everyone went to his own town to be registered. 4 So Joseph also went up from the town of Nazareth in Galilee to Judea, to the city of David called Bethlehem, because he was of the house and family line of David. 5 He went to be registered with Mary, who was promised in marriage to him, and who was expecting a child. 6 While they were there, the time came for her to deliver her child. 7 And she gave birth to her firstborn son and wrapped him in strips of cloth and laid him in a manger, because there was no place for them in the inn."

Romans 8:31–32, 38–39, "What then shall we say about these things? If God is for us, who can be against us? 32 Indeed, he who did not spare his own Son, but gave him up for us all—how will he not also, along with him, freely give us all things? … 38 For I am convinced that neither death, nor life, nor angels, nor heavenly rulers, nor things that are present, nor things to come, nor powers, 39 nor height, nor depth, nor anything else in creation will be able to separate us from the love of God in Christ Jesus our Lord."

Through this entire journey, we've learned that no matter how many rebellions there were, God's plan for His family could not be stopped. Jesus was always there through it all, guiding God's Remnant, so that one day God could send His Son to be the Savior of the Cosmos. Then, now, and tomorrow, nothing can separate us from the love of God.

Questions

1. Why did Mary and Joseph have to travel to Bethlehem? Joseph's family line from David was from there. And they had to register there for taxes.

2. Where did Jesus sleep? In a manger.

3. Why was Jesus born in a manger? There was no room for them in the inn.

4. Why did God send His Son to earth? He loves the cosmos.

5. Can anything separate us from God's love? No.

Prayer

Dear God, thank You for loving us and sending Your Son to redeem us. Thank you that nothing can separate us from You. Help us to have faith in Your promises and to obey you. Amen.

Songs

"Infant Holy, Infant Lowly", "Come, Thou long expected Jesus"